Domesday

John Fines and Jon Nichol

Basil Blackwell

1 The Norman Conquest

A magnificent victory – Duke William triumphs over King Harold

might have read the headlines in *The Norman Times* of October 1066.

England's darkest hour – King Harold dead

is how *The Saxon Chronicle* might have told the same story.

Of course, in 1066 there were no newspapers. News spread slowly, by letter or word of mouth, at the speed of a running man or a galloping horse. On the evening of 14 October 1066 only a few people knew of the battle just fought near Hastings in England, between Duke William of Normandy and Harold, King of England, see **A**.

What might it have been like for you to have been present at the battle **B**? Imagine that the fight is over. Duke William pushes back his sweat-stained helmet, and looks around. Broken weapons litter the ground. Gashed and bloody bodies lie in heaps. William hears the groans of the wounded and dying, and the neighing of horses. The smell of cooking drifts across from a newly-lit fire.

William asks the leaders of his army to join him and advise him on his next move. Look at the list of things they might think about, **C**. If you had been one of William's chief men, what advice would you give him? You begin to argue fiercely with William about the problems you face. It is getting late, so you pitch your tents. That night you go on talking about what the Norman army should do. In fact, you stay at Hastings for five days before making your next move.

(A) The Norman Conquest

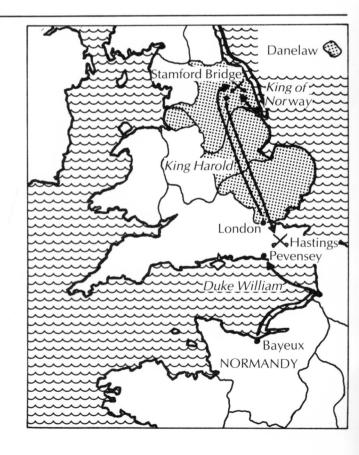

The Norman Conquest
1064 Harold, Earl of Wessex, promises to back Duke William as the next King of England on King Edward's death.
1066 *5 January* King Edward dies.
6 January Harold becomes King.
Earl Edwin of Mercia and his brother Morcar, Earl of Northumberland, are not loyal to Harold.
Summer The King of Norway invades England.
25 September Harold kills him at the Battle of Stamford Bridge.
28 September Duke William of Normandy lands with his army. Harold rushes to fight him.
14 October Battle of Hastings. Harold killed.

B The Battle of Hastings, from the Bayeux Tapestry

© Problems facing the Norman army.

1 You have sailed from Normandy – a dukedom one-tenth the size of England. The Channel cuts you off from home. In and around Normandy you have lots of enemies waiting to seize your lands if you are stuck in England.

2 William has only been able to raise 800 Norman knights to invade England. The rest of the army are hired men – fighting for money and booty. They cannot be trusted.

3 You cannot trust the other Normans. Even William's family might rebel. All Normans hate taking orders.

4 Duke William is a bastard. His mother, the daughter of a tanner, never got around to marrying his father. (In those days this mattered for Dukes and Kings. Their subjects were more likely to obey them if they were the sons of married parents.)

5 Although William has killed Harold, the rulers of Mercia and Northumbria may raise strong armies to fight him.

6 William has no idea of the geography of England. He does not know where places are, or how far apart they might be.

7 None of you speaks English. You have no idea of how the country is ruled.

8 None of you knows who owns what land, what the laws of the country are, or how the king raises money to pay his troops.

ACTIVITY

1 Draw a map of England between your home and either London or York, whichever is the furthest away. Mark on it towns you have heard of, and rivers, hills, forests, lakes, marshes and the coast. Do this *without* looking at an atlas. Plan out how you would make the journey there on foot. Compare your map and ideas with other members of your class. What does this suggest about the problems William faced after the Battle of Hastings?

2 Find out what you can about the Battle of Hastings. In groups, divide the story up into scenes from the death of King Edward to the battle itself. Then draw each scene in cartoon form, and use the cartoons to make a display around the room.

3 a As a class talk through the problems which faced William with your teacher.
b Split into groups and sort out your advice about what to do next. Report back to the rest of the class.
c When you report back, listen carefully to what the other groups have to say. Notice how their ideas differ from yours.
d Is some advice better than others? Are there some problems you cannot solve?

4 Find as many pictures and stories of fighting today as you can. Use these to help you say what it might have been like to have fought at the Battle of Hastings as a Norman knight.

3

2 William Rules, 1066–85

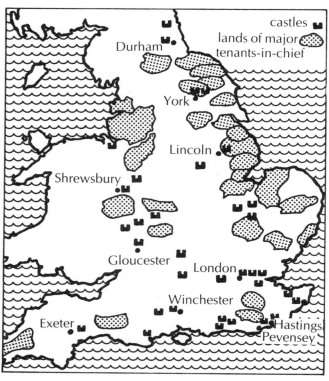

(A) How William took over England

his strongest followers in places where there was danger – like the Welsh borders. Here the Normans built many castles, see **A**.

There could well be Norman castles near your school or home – see **C**. If you live in England, William would have given land in your area to his knights. You can see how he did this on pages 6–7.

Castle -

(C) The symbol for a castle on Ordnance Survey maps

King William faced many revolts and risings in his reign, **D**. There were three main kinds: Anglo-Saxon risings (like those of Hereward the Wake and Edric the Wild); revolts of Norman barons and members of William's family; and foreign invasions (Welsh, Scottish, Irish, Norwegian or Danish armies would often join up with his other enemies).

After Hastings, King William and his barons made up their minds to advance slowly on London. At Christmas in 1066 William was crowned King of England at Westminster Abbey in London. The conquest of England was a long, hard job. As William pushed forward across England, he gave the lands of King Harold and his **thanes** (followers) to his own men, see **A**. The lands of men who fought at Hastings went first. **B** is a letter William wrote to 'Athelmaer the Bishop and Ralph the Earl and to all my knights'. It contains clues as to how the Normans seized Anglo-Saxon lands:

(B) **❝** I give you to know that I will that Abbot Baldwin hand to me all the land which those men held who belonged to St Edmund's soke (district) and who stood in battle against me and there were slain. **❞**

William did not give the land to his barons all at once. There were still two major Anglo-Saxon land holders left 20 years after the Battle of Hastings. William was keen to give land to

(D) **Risings against William I 1066–85**

1067	Rebellion led by Eustace of Boulogne at Dover. Edric the Wild leads the first of his uprisings in Herefordshire.
1068	Uprising at Exeter.
1069	Edric's second rising, with Welsh princes; burns Shrewsbury. Danes in Humber. Trouble at York and in the Isle of Axholm.
1070	Hereward the Wake leads rising at Ely.
1072	William involved in fighting with the Scots.
1075	Roger Earl of Hereford, Waltheof Earl of Northumberland and Ralf Earl of East Anglia rise. Danish raid on York.
1080	Rising at Gateshead. Expedition into Scotland.
1081	Expedition to St David's (Wales).
1082	William arrests his half-brother, Odo of Bayeux.
1085	Danes, Norwegians and Flemish plan a joint invasion (which doesn't in fact take place).

E   A Norman army 'wasting' a village

Domesday Book entries for your area might contain clues about how William dealt with these risings. He crushed them ruthlessly. The Norman army killed, burnt, pillaged and wrecked wherever it went. In 1069 William put down a rising in the North of England with great brutality (see page 15).

Look at Domesday Book to see whether you can trace William the Conqueror's footsteps as his army marched through your area. The opening lines of each entry (see pages 14–15) might show that William's forces marched through and 'wasted' the region, **E**. A big drop in the value of villages between 1066 and 1087 could mean that William had devastated the countryside.

ACTIVITY

1 *Either* Use **E**, and any pictures you can find of modern armies wrecking homes and villages, to draw a picture of how a Norman army might have devastated a village near your home. Add this picture to the cartoon on page 3.
or Discuss in pairs what a villein might tell you about what happened when the Normans devastated his village. Mention: the rising, news of the army's approach, flight, panic, scene on your return. (Use page 15 to help you.)

2 Discuss why you think William decided to 'waste' villages and towns. Do you think he was wise to do this? Why? (Remember we are talking about being 'wise' not about being 'good'.)

3 *Domesday work.*
  a Find out if there are Norman castles in your area. Often they will be marked on your local Ordnance Survey map – see **C**.
  b Draw up a list of the Normans who held land in your area, and the Saxons whom they replaced. What do you think happened to the Saxons? (Use page 15.)

3 The Feudal System

Have you ever been to a wedding? If the service was in a church you might have seen the bride take an oath to obey her husband. King William made his barons, knights and bishops take oaths to obey him. Each Domesday entry contains a clue about these oaths or promises. Every entry tells us that *someone* holds a *certain place* – for example: *Earl Roger* holds *Montgomery*.

This means that Earl Roger holds his land from King William. In return for his land he has sworn an oath of loyalty to the King. William made direct grants of land holdings to his **tenants-in-chief**, like Earl Roger. A tenant-in-chief's land was called his **fief**.

In return for his land, Earl Roger had to provide a number of knights to fight in the King's army or to man his castles. The knights had to be fully trained and armed, ready to serve the King for up to 40 days a year. To train and keep a knight cost a huge amount of money.

In turn the tenant-in-chief gave land to his knights. Each knight promised to fight for the tenant-in-chief when asked. The knights gave land to the peasants. In return, they worked on the knight's farm. This pattern of land holding is called the **feudal system**, **A**.

1 Draw a feudal pyramid for the fief of William de Braose showing
  – King William
  – William de Braose
  – The under-tenants

(A) How the feudal system worked

The King, owner of all the land

gives land to tenants--in-chief to hold, their **fiefs**. King William protects them against their enemies.

tenants-in-chief provide King William with knights for his army

Tenants-in-chief (2–300)

grant land to their under-tenants, mainly knights. Their land (**manors**) supports them. The tenant-in-chief also provides military protection for their knights.

the under-tenants fight for the tenant-in-chief when called upon

Under-tenants (4–5000)

give land in the vills to their peasants to hold. They protect their peasants from attack from armed bands. Also, they provide law and order through the manor court.

peasants do **boon service** on the land at the manor's demesne farm

The peasants (1 250 000)

After 1066 King William had a lot of land to give out. Domesday Book does not cover all of England — some areas are missing, as well as big towns like London. Even so, it lists 13 000 **vills** or settlements. How many vills might there have been within your area? If you have your local Domesday entries you will notice at once that more than one man might hold a vill. Often a vill was split up between two or more land holders. We call each person's land holding a **manor**. You can get an idea of how the system worked if you look at Domesday Sussex, **B**.

Domesday Sussex. We have counted 338 vills mentioned in Domesday Book for Sussex, split up into 537 holdings or manors. In Sussex the King had 15 tenants-in-chief: the Archbishop of Canterbury; two bishops; five abbots; two counts; one earl; two barons; two knights. (King William also kept the best land for himself.)

The tenants-in-chief promised to supply William with knights. How did they do this?

This is how one tenant-in-chief managed: William de Braose was put in charge of the defence of one part of Sussex. He based himself on Bramber castle — you can still see its ruins today. King William gave William de Braose 57 holdings. The whole fief was worth £357.55 pence. That was a huge amount of money — the *whole* of England was only worth £73 000. William de Braose kept 10 holdings for himself worth £216.75. He granted 47 holdings worth £178.80 to others, in the same way that King William had granted them to him. Amongst these land holders were 14 knights. They paid homage to William de Braose and promised to do him knight service in return for their land. William de Braose's land came from Anglo-Saxon thanes. One of their holdings had belonged to Earl Gyrth. At the Battle of Hastings William the Conqueror had slain the Earl after he had killed the Conqueror's horse.

BECOMING A LAND HOLDER AND KNIGHT

How did someone become a knight? As a form let's take part in a play about granting fiefs and knighthoods. Read through the stages below. Then act out what would have happened.

1 Choose who shall be the tenant-in-chief of your area (it could be your teacher).

2 Look at a map of vills in your area (see page 12). Decide which place or places you would have liked to hold from your local tenant-in-chief. Write down which holdings you might bid for. Write these on a piece of paper.

3 Think how you might persuade the tenant-in-chief that you can be trusted.

4 Go to the tenant-in-chief and bargain with him. Show him respect — if you do not, you will get nothing. Remember, the tenant-in-chief would like to keep the best vills for himself. Tell him what you can offer him in return for the land he might grant you.

5 When the tenant-in-chief has decided who shall hold which vill (or shares of it/them) you must swear homage to him.

6 Swearing homage
- kneel before the tenant-in-chief with your hands held up together as if in prayer
- beside you will stand your witnesses. They will be the local bishop and a baron or court official of the tenant-in-chief
- the tenant-in-chief places his hands around yours (making a sandwich of them)
- then you promise to be honest and true. To obey the tenant-in-chief and supply him with knight service and other soldiers and supplies he might want
- to remind you to keep your promise, the tenant-in-chief gives a light blow (remember the Queen still *dubs* knights with her sword)

7 After the tenant-in-chief has sworn in his knights, they can make out a charter of their rights to their lands, and the promises of service they have made to the tenant-in-chief.

8 In turn, the tenant-in-chief can make out his charter of promises to the King, and the nature of the holdings which he has received from him.

4 King William and Domesday, 1085

A meeting of the King's council in Saxon times. Meetings of William's council would have been similar.

How did William rule England and Normandy? Each year he held three great meetings of his council of earls, barons, knights, archbishops, bishops and abbots, see **A**. He called the council members to his court at Winchester (Easter), Westminster (Whitsuntide) and Gloucester (Christmas). Look at a map to see why he chose those three places to meet.

Any noble who had a problem could bring it to one of these three meetings for the King and his council to solve. Within a few years of the Norman Conquest, many problems arose over the grants of land which William had made and over other matters, see **B**. For example, a noble like William de Braose (see page 7) might claim that the Archbishop of Canterbury had seized some of his lands. Or, he might say that William was asking for too many knights service. You can guess the sort of thing: after a fight in the playground the teacher asks what happened – think of the many answers he gets!

How would William sort out rows over fiefs, the value of manors, the number of knights

service owed, the ownership of lands? Remember that he would have to rely on what people could remember of the service of homage. How well can you remember things from years ago?

Between 1066 and 1085 a lot of witnesses would have died, and some bits of writing would have been lost. When the Normans wrote down details of land holdings and the knight service owed, they called it a **charter**. Some people owned charters in 1085, some didn't, some had lost theirs, while some had even forged them!

In 1085 William told his mid-winter council meeting at Gloucester that he was going to carry out a survey of England to help solve rows over land, tax owed and knight service. The council would work out a way to write down full details of what it could find out about the people, animals, buildings and land of England. A record would be made of who owned what and how, what it was worth, and what they owed to whom. William knew his

B

1079	The same year King William fought against his son Robert outside Normandy . . . King William was wounded there, and his horse killed under him. His son William was also wounded and many men slain **C**.
1081	In this year the King led his levies (knights doing service) into Wales . . .
1082	And in this year was a great famine . . .
1083	In this year a great row broke out at Glastonbury between the Abbot Thurstan and his monks . . .
1085	In this year men reported that Cnut, King of Denmark . . . was on his way here, determined to conquer this country. When King William learnt of this . . . he returned to England with a vast army of horses and foot from France . . . It was so huge that men wondered how this land could feed such an army. The king, however, had the army spread over the whole country, boarding them with each of his vassals according to the wealth of his estate.

(from: *The Anglo-Saxon Chronicle*)

council would obey. He was a tough and ruthless leader, and many people were afraid of him. This is how one Norman monk described him:

D ❢ *He was a very stern and violent man, so that no one dared act against his will. He put his earls into chains who acted against his will. He threw bishops out of their sees and abbots from their abbacies, and put them into prison . . . He did not spare his own brother who was called Odo . . . When the king was in Normandy then Odo was master of this country, and he* (the king) *put him in prison . . . The good safety he* (the king) *made in this country is not to be forgotten. So that, any honest man could travel over his kingdom without injury with his bosom full of gold.* ❢

When news of the survey seeped out, people were shocked. The monk who wrote the *Anglo-Saxon Chronicle* tells us:

E ❢ *So very thoroughly did he have the enquiry carried out there was not a single "hide", not one virgate of land, not even, it is shameful to record it, but it did not seem shameful for him to do – not even one ox, nor*

C King William's son, William, who was killed in 1079

one cow, nor one pig which escaped notice in his survey. ❢

William found out so much about the vills and towns of England and the people who lived there that they called his survey the *Book of Judgement* – or *Domesday Book*. ('Domesday' is when the Normans believed the world would end: then they would be judged and go to heaven or hell.)

ACTIVITY

1 As a group, or on your own, draw a cartoon showing: one of the scenes in **B**; a cartoon about William's character; the 1085 Gloucester council meeting. Add this to your work on pages 3 and 5.

2 Think of a problem about your own lands to bring to the Council to discuss. How would you persuade them to judge it in your favour?

3 As if you were at the Gloucester meeting which decided to carry out the Domesday survey write *five* sentences about what went on. Then whisper this message to your neighbour, who has to pass it on to his/her neighbour, and so on around the class. How has it changed by the end of its journey? What does this suggest about **D**, and the spread of news about the King's enquiry?

5 The King's Enquiry

How was the enquiry to be carried out? William wanted a quick answer to the questions he had asked about England. So, his council split England up into seven areas or **circuits**. A team of commissioners was sent to tour each area. They had the power to ask as many questions as they wanted. To make sure that they did a good job William told them he would send along another team later to check their work.

It is likely that each team took from the King's records as many papers as it could find to help it – papers such as charters and tax lists. When a team reached the county town of a shire, the chief local man of the King, the **sheriff**, would have dug out more papers for it. The sheriff would also be present at all the meetings of the commissioners. When ready, the commissioners sent out orders to every vill and town for the following men to attend the meetings of the commission, which would collect facts for the King's survey:

  tenants-in-chief *or* their stewards;
  knights *or* their stewards;
  the priest; the reeve (a villein chosen by the villagers to be in charge of them for a year);
  six villeins.

Each shire was split up into regions called **hundreds** (or **wapentakes** in the old Danelaw see page 2). From each hundred came a jury of four Frenchmen and four Englishmen to check that the answers about vills in their hundred were correct.

Think of the problems which the commissioners faced. In 1086 England was a country of many tribes and races. Celtic was still the normal tongue of the Welsh borders, Cornwall and West Devon. In much of northern England Danish and Norse settlers farmed the land. In the rest of England survived the laws, customs and habits of speech of the Anglo-Saxon tribes who had settled 500 or 600 years before. Even today local speech and dialects are hard to follow – so you can imagine what it must have been like for the commissioners!

The commissioners were hard-working and clever men. They got the job done in record time. By the end of 1086 they had sent in their answers to the King's chief clerk, Sampson, at Winchester. His job was to sort out the hundreds of pages of writing and to put it together in a simple form – Domesday Book (see pages 12–14).

The King's Questions

Pretend it is a hot summer day in 1086. You are a peasant living in a village which belongs to a Norman knight. As you work in the fields you see a stranger ride down the dusty track into the village. He climbs down from his horse and enters the hut of the village steward. The steward runs the knight's farm or **demesne**. A rumour spreads through the field that the stranger has brought a message from King William.

After the day's work has ended the steward calls a village meeting to explain what the messenger said. The steward tells you that King William has ordered that every village shall send the priest, reeve and six peasants to meet the King's chief man in the county – his **shire reeve** or **sheriff**. The shire reeve will ask each village's men questions to find out about their village. The King wants to find out about each village: who owns it, how much land it has, how many people, animals and property and what it is worth each year. *The King's Questions* are the same for every village in England. The King's orders are that all the villages of England shall answer his questions.

You are chosen as one of the six peasants who will help reply to the King's Questions.

ACTIVITY

1 Draw a cartoon strip showing the story of *either*

a How the Domesday enquiry was carried out – from splitting England up into seven areas to the calling of the people of a hundred to the local enquiry.

b How the news reached the village and spread around it – from the sighting of the King's messenger to the reading of the King's questions.

2 As a class, discuss the problems which the teams of commissioners might have met. Draw up a list of them and by the side of each say how the problem might have been solved.

3 Split into groups of up to five. Each of you take the role of *one* of the following group members:
   – tenant-in-chief or knight
   – priest
   – steward
   – villein or miller.

Read through the King's questions. As if you were one of the people in the list explain why you think the King wants to know these things. Why might your views differ?

What is the manor called?
_____

Who held it in the time of King Edward?
_____

Who now holds it?
1   2
_____

How many hides?   How many ploughs?
_____   _____

How many hides in demesne?
_____

How many ploughs on demesne?
_____

How many villeins?
_____

How many bordars?
_____

How many cottars?
_____

How many slaves?
_____

How many freemen?
_____

How many socmen?
_____

How much wood?
_____

How much meadow?
_____

How much pasture?
_____

How much was it worth in the time of King Edward?
_____

How much was it worth when King William gave it?
_____

How much is it worth now?
_____

How much extra might it be worth?
_____

How much land had or has each free man or socman?
_____

How many sheep?
_____

How many swine?
_____

How many horses?
_____

How many cows?
_____

How many goats?
_____

How many mills?
_____

How many fish ponds?
_____

How much has been added or taken away?
_____

6 Domesday!

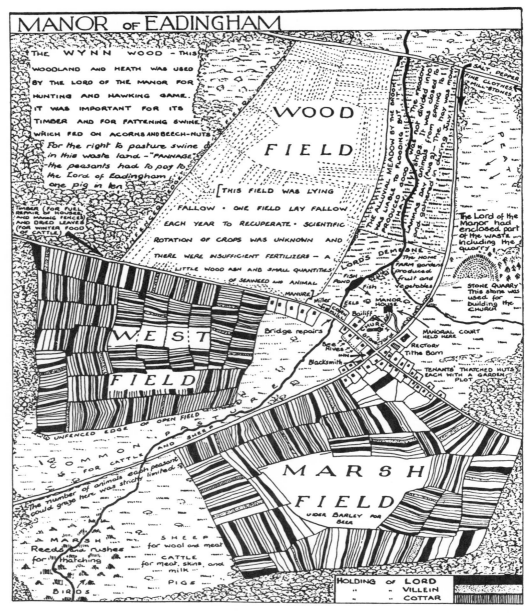

MANOR OF EADINGHAM

THE WYNN WOOD — THIS WOODLAND AND HEATH WAS USED BY THE LORD OF THE MANOR FOR HUNTING AND HAWKING GAME. IT WAS IMPORTANT FOR ITS TIMBER AND FOR FATTENING SWINE, WHICH FED ON ACORNS AND BEECH-NUTS. For the right to pasture swine in this waste land — "PANNAGE" — the peasants had to pay to the Lord of Eadingham one pig in ten.

TIMBER (FOR FUEL REPAIR OF HOUSES AND MAKING FENCES) AND DRIED LEAVES (FOR WINTER FOOD OF CATTLE).

WOOD FIELD

[THIS FIELD WAS LYING FALLOW. ONE FIELD LAY FALLOW EACH YEAR TO RECUPERATE. SCIENTIFIC ROTATION OF CROPS WAS UNKNOWN AND THERE WERE INSUFFICIENT FERTILIZERS — A LITTLE WOOD ASH AND SMALL QUANTITIES OF SEAWEED AND ANIMAL MANURE]

THE ALLUVIAL MEADOW BY THE BROOK PRODUCED GOOD HAY BUT WAS LIABLE TO FLOODING

The Lord of the Manor had enclosed part of the waste — including the quarry.

LORDS DEMESNE — The Home FARM garden produced fruit and vegetables

STONE QUARRY This stone was used for building the CHURCH

SALT PEPPER FINE CLOTHES MILL-STONES

WEST FIELD

Miller

Bailiff

EELS

Fish Pond

Fish

MANOR HOUSE

MANORIAL COURT HELD HERE

RECTORY

Tithe Barn

Bridge repairs

Bee Hives

Blacksmith

TENANTS' THATCHED HUTS EACH WITH A GARDEN PLOT

UNFENCED EDGE OF OPEN FIELD

COMMON — FOR CATTLE AND SHEEP

The number of animals each peasant could graze here was strictly limited

MARSH FIELD UNDER BARLEY FOR BEER

MARSH Reeds and rushes for thatching

SHEEP for wool and meat

CATTLE for meat, skins, and milk

PIGS

BIRDS

HOLDING	OF	LORD
"	"	VILLEIN
"	"	COTTAR

(A) A Norman vill – The manor of Eadingham

Within a ten-mile radius of your school there would have been many vills in 1086. Use an Ordnance Survey map or a map of Domesday villages to find out where they were.

Split up into groups of three or four. Between you, choose one of the vills in your area (or you could take one you chose on page 11). What might your vill have been like in 1086?

A shows what a typical Norman vill might have been like. Now draw a plan of your vill.

To help you, follow these steps:

a If there is a Domesday entry for your vill, read it. To help you understand the entry, look at page 14, and use the Index inside the back of this book to find out where to look for more information.

b Make notes about where you think the following features should be on your map (look up the page numbers, in brackets, to find out more about them):

manor house (20); church (28); villeins' houses (21); mill (24); fish ponds (24); hills (3); streams/ rivers/marsh (3); woods (17); meadows (16); tracks (3); open fields – up to 5 (16).
Mark on the knight's demesne and the priest's glebe (18). There might also be a castle (26). Make notes on the kinds and number of animals (23).

c Talk about your answers in **b**. Now use your notes to help you draw the plan of your vill. You could make three or four maps, or you may decide to draw a joint one.

When you have drawn your maps, split up the class into two groups – commissioners and people from the vills – so that there is one commissioner for every two vills. (Remember, every vill was represented by a team of people.)

The commissioners order the villagers to come to a meeting in the shire town. The sheriff (this could be your teacher) calls the meeting to order. The commissioners have brought the list of questions (see page 10). Each commissioner uses this list to ask questions about two vills. He can ask the people from each vill either as a group or as separate witnesses.

When the enquiries are over the sheriff can choose a jury of eight people from the villagers to check into any of the answers given to the commissioners' questions. They have the power to ask the villagers any questions they like, to get at the truth.

ACTIVITY

1 Make up a diary entry about the Domesday enquiry. Mention:
- rumours about the survey – the official messenger;
- choosing people to go to the meeting;
- gathering information – drawing your map;
- travelling to the meeting;
- the commissioners' questions – your answers;
- how you felt during the meeting;
- what the jury asked.

2 Discuss what the acting out has told you about the Domesday enquiry. How much trust can we place on facts in the Domesday Book? How might we check those facts?

3 Mount your own maps of the vills on a large wall map of your area.

7 Domesday Book

Each group of commissioners wrote down the replies they got to their questions about the vills and towns of the shires they visited, on sheets of parchment. They sent their writings to the King's chief clerk, Sampson. At Winchester, Sampson wrote out the replies in a standard form.

Sampson left much local detail out of his final copy. We know details are missing because some local commissioners' findings still survive. These are full of details which are missing from the bare entries in Domesday Book. Sampson wrote Domesday Book in Latin **A**. Often he put names and facts in a shortened form to save space.

How can you go about sorting out the meaning of the entries in Domesday Book about your area? How can we put the flesh and blood back on to the dry bones of history which Domesday Book contains? How can we put life back into the body? You need to build up in your mind a picture of what the vills of Domesday and their people might have been like. We have got to use our imaginations – but imagination linked to the facts that we can find out about life in 1086.

On the next page there is a typical example, Hambledon. It is a small village in Hampshire near the English Channel. The numbers suggest how you might make sense of it and entries like it.

(A) Part of a Domesday entry

William de Percy (1) holds Hambledon (2). He came by it along with his wife (3). Alwin (4) held it from King Edward (5). It was then taxed as 8 hides (6). There is land for 3 ploughs (7). There is 1 plough on the demesne (8). Also there are 6 villeins (9) and 6 bordars (10) with 2 ploughs (7). There are 2 serfs (11) and a mill (12) worth 12 pence (13). There is a woodland (14) worth 4 swine (15). In Edward's reign (5) it was worth 4 pounds (16) as it is now (17). When it first came to its present lord (18) it was worth 3 pounds (16) 14 pence (13).

Solving the Domesday Book riddle

First Look in the *Index* at the back of this book to see if there are any terms which you do not know. Look up the pages the index shows to find out about them.

Second Work through the Hambledon entry, to give you an idea of how you might do your own work. The numbers refer to the text for Hambledon.

Hambledon Number	Notes	Index
1	the name of the Norman tenant-in-chief (note there is no sub-tenant here)	18
2	the name of the manor	6
3	the wife of the tenant-in-chief	18
4	Alwin, the Anglo-Saxon who held the manor in 1066	15
5	King Edward died in 1066	2
6	hides, a measurement of land value for taxation	9
7	ploughs – for ploughing the land	16
8	demesne – the farm of the lord of the manor	18
9	villeins, peasants in the vill	25
10	bordars, peasants in the vill	25
11	serfs, peasants in the vill	25
12	mill – for grinding corn	24
13	pence, a unit of money	
14	woodland – area of woodland or forest	17
15	swine – pigs	17
16	pounds – a measure of money	
17	now = 1086	12
18	present lord = William de Percy	

Using Domesday Book

You should now have some idea of what Domesday Book (see **B**) was about: why King William had it made, how it was carried out and how it reflects the feudal system. The rest of this book will try and unlock the meaning of the extracts. It will also help you fill in the gaps – where there is nothing written down about what must have been present in the vill when the commissioners wrote down the villagers' evidence. For example, almost all of the Domesday Book entries contain nothing about animals. Yet, we know that the commissioners wrote down details of all vills' animals in their enquiry.

Our first piece of detective work is about the *first* part of each Domesday entry – who held the land before 1066 and who holds it now. These entries help throw light on what happened to the Anglo-Saxons who owned the country's vills and towns before the Norman Conquest.

B Domesday Book

ACTIVITY

Look at either a Domesday entry for your area, or the entry for Hambledon.

a What problems might you have in sorting out what the evidence means?
b How were the facts in the entry gathered (see pages 10–11)?
c What happened to these facts between the commissioners' enquiry and when they were written down in Domesday Book?
d How much trust can you place on the entry?
e How would you check if the facts were true?

8 What Happened to the Anglo-Saxons?

Look out for stories about Israel and the Middle East on television. In them you may hear about *refugees* – people who have had to leave their homes and land. After 1066 many Anglo-Saxons became refugees. Domesday Book contains lots of clues about what happened. The Hecham entry is like most others:

(A) *Peter de Valence holds in demesne Hecham, which Haldane, a freeman, held in the time of King Edward.*

The time of King Edward was before 1066. What happened to Haldane and the thousands of other Anglo-Saxon land holders after 1066?

Some managed to rent back their lands from their new Norman land holders, like the Anglo-Saxon Aelric of Marsh Gibbon, in Buckinghamshire. He now held his land 'heavily and miserably'. Others fled – to Scotland, Flanders and Scandinavia. A few even ended up in the bodyguard of the great Emperor of Byzantium at Constantinople. Only two Anglo-Saxon land holders were left in England in 1086.

There were many Anglo-Saxon risings against William's rule throughout his reign (see pages 4–5). William used great force to crush these rebellions. Then he 'wasted' or devastated the areas where the rebels lived. Not a building or crop was left standing, not a person or animal left alive.

Think what it must have been like to have been a peasant in an area as news spread of the approach of the wrecking Norman army. A stream of refugees would flood through your village . . . In 1069 William 'wasted' or harried the North of England, which had risen up against him. In Yorkshire his army burned between a third and a half of all vills.

After Edric the Wild's rising William 'wasted' the North Midlands. The Abbot of Evesham sadly recalled the crowds of panic-stricken refugees – old men, women and children, – who flocked into the town. There they died in droves. Domesday Book contains clues about wasting and devastation. For example, an entry might show a sharp drop in the value of land, like this:

(B) *Herewulf holds Netherfield from the Count . . . Value before 1066, 100s. Now 50s, it was wasted.*

Why has there been this huge fall in value?

An entry might also record that there are no longer enough plough teams to plough the land:

(C) *Earl Harold held Crowhurst. Then it answered for 6 hides: now 3 hides. Land for 22 ploughs. Walter, son of Lambert, holds it from the count. He has 2 ploughs in Lordship. 12 villagers and 6 cottagers have 12 ploughs . . . One Walo holds ½ hide and 2 virgates. 3 villagers with 1 plough there.*

The simplest record of 'wasting' is when the entry reads: *wasta* or *wasta est* (waste or wasted).

But, take care in reading too much into these entries. There are many other reasons for 'waste' – such as Danish invasions and the outbreak of disease or some other natural disaster.

1 The Anglo-Saxons were good at making up poems to show how sad they were. As if you were an Anglo-Saxon thane who had fled to Scandinavia after an uprising, write a poem about what has happened to you and your people since 1066.

2 Look in Domesday Book for your area and see if there are any signs of 'wasting'. If there are, look at map **A** on page 4 and try and work out what the reasons for the 'wasting' might have been.

3 Write the orders to a Norman knight and band of soldiers telling them to devastate the vills in your area. Give full details of what you want the band of 20 soldiers to do.

9 The Land

Look at the map of your vill, or map **A** on page 12. How much of the land in the vill, was:

kind of land	Domesday terms	measures (see page 11)
Meadow	meadow	
Rough grazing		
Ploughland for crops	hides, virgates, ploughs	
Woodland for pigs	woodland	
Forest for hunting	forest	

The land use in a vill near where you live would depend on what the countryside was like, climate, how it had been farmed before 1066 and its history from 1066–86. Land use differed sharply from one part of England to another. A vill in the Fens was a total contrast to one on Dartmoor. Fields, houses, ways of farming, crops and animals were all different.

Domesday Book entries contain thousands of clues about land use in 1086. The word **plough** tells us that the peasants ploughed the land so as to sow and harvest their crops. Most Norman farmland was used for crops, that is, arable farming. The peasants grew wheat and rye to make black bread; barley to brew beer; peas and beans for vegetables. Often the fields in 1086, or land on their edges, had been cleared in the past 50 years. Gangs of peasants would have chopped or burned down the woods, so there would be old tree stumps and rocks to clear.

Can you think what it was like to plough the land? Imagine a great, heavy plough with up to eight lumbering oxen pulling it **A**, and men standing on the plough to make it stick in the soil. Lots of shouting and swearing!

Next, the peasants would have to make the large clods of ploughed earth ready for sowing the seed. The **harrow**, **B**, helped, but there was much back-breaking work with spades and hoes. Women and children spent many freezing hours breaking up the lumps of soil to make fine seed beds, and picking up stones.

While the crops grew the peasant family would clear weeds, nettles and brambles. There were no weedkillers in those days! You might have had a job as a bird scarer – spending the days in the fields shooing away crows and pigeons who were greedy to eat the growing crops. In the late summer came the harvest, which meant working with sickle and scythe to gather in the ripe grain while the good weather lasted. Then winter, and time to plough again. All hard work, but it had to be done, or you would starve. In 1086 as much land was ploughed in England as in 1900.

The Normans grew crops elsewhere, too. The lord of the manor, priest and peasants had their own gardens. For **cottars** (see page 26) this was all the land they had. Some vills had lots of gardens. There were 23 at Holywell near Oxford. There must have been plenty of orchards, too, although Domesday Book did not bother to mention any. There are entries, however, for more than 40 *vineyards*. The Normans were keen to make their own wine. They had no wish to pay the huge cost of shipping it across from France.

(A) Ploughing

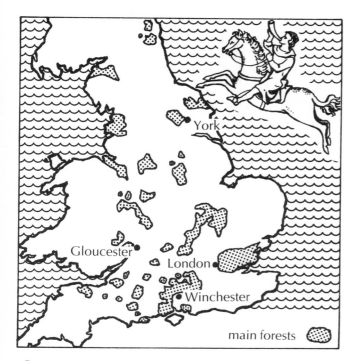

C The royal forests, about 100 years after Domesday

Vills measured their woodland according to how it was used. Some said, 'Our woodland will produce so much timber each year.' Others said, 'Our woods will feed so many pigs.'

Forests were a special kind of woodland, **C**. Forest was kept for the King and his knights to hunt in – chasing deer on horseback kept them fighting fit. Looking after the forest gave jobs to some village people – as gamekeepers, huntsmen and foresters. But many people hated the forests. In the forest, the peasants had to obey forest law, which said that no-one must disturb the game. Poachers would be whipped, or even hung. The story of Robin Hood reminds us how much the peasants loathed the forests and forest law.

The cows, oxen, horses, sheep, goats and donkeys needed grassland to graze on. In return for their animals' grazing the peasants had to work for the lord of the manor, or pay him **dues** instead. Sometimes their sheep would run wild on moor or heath. On the rough grassland you would also find rabbits – a very good source of meat and furs for the poor peasant.

The biggest problem for the Normans was what to do with their animals in the winter. In autumn the peasants killed off many of their animals and salted down their meat to preserve it. They kept some animals for breeding – and these needed food through the long cold winter months when nothing grew. This is where the meadow came in handy. Meadow land grew hay for winter feed. It was worth a lot of money. It fetched three times as much as ploughland. Look at your village to see how much pasture and meadow there was, and what it was worth.

The most common type of land was woodland. You could put your pigs in the woods, and they fed themselves. At Waltham they had room for 2000 pigs or swine. From the woods you also got wood for building fences or houses, and making wooden tools – and fuel for the fire. If you wanted more ploughland you could clear or **assart** the woods on the edge of the fields.

ACTIVITY

1 Make out a chart, in either drawn or written form, to show how the land of your vill might have been split up and what it was used for. Discuss each heading in class – you can have a 'brain-storming' session to see how many things you can think of for raw materials, use, and what made into.

Land	Amount	Raw materials from	What used for	What made
Arable Grazing Meadow Woodland Forest				

2 In groups discuss how you would measure your local woodland. Give reasons for your final choice of method. (If you think you have a good idea, think of how the commissioners might have envied you.)

3 Find a book about the adventures of Robin Hood in the royal forest. Read about them, then re-tell one of the stories from the viewpoint of *either* a gamekeeper trying to catch the poachers *or* the Sheriff of Nottingham.

10 King, Tenant-in-chief, Knight and Priest

Three people whom Domesday Book mentions may well not have lived in your vill or local town – King William, the tenant-in-chief and the subholder. All three are recorded in the typical entry for Singleton, Sussex:

(A) *Earl Roger* (tenant-in-chief) *holds Singleton in lordship* (from King William) . . . *A church in whose lands lie 3 hides and 1 virgate of this land. The clergy* (under-tenants) *have 2 ploughs and 5 smallholders. Payne holds 1 hide of this manor from the Earl; William 1 hide, Geoffrey 2 hides* (under-tenants). *What the clergy hold £8. What the men-at-arms hold £14.*

The King appears in some way on every page of Domesday Book. Out of the wealth of England in 1086, about £73 000, King William took about £11 000. That is about 15 per cent, i.e. £15 out of every £100! This was twice what King Edward had taken. No wonder many Anglo-Saxons thought that King William was greedy.

(B) *The King gave his land as dearly for rent as he possibly could. Then came some other and bid more than the other had before given. The King let it to the man who had bid most of all. And he didn't care how the reeves sinned to get it* (money) *from the poor men, or how many crimes they carried out.*

The tenants-in-chief were soldiers (earls, counts, barons and knights) or great churchmen (archbishops, bishops or abbots). The churchmen were soldiers as well, with their own forces of knights. Many of the tenants-in-chief had fought at Hastings. They often held many manors. Map **C** shows the lands of one tenant-in-chief, Gilbert of Clare. The tenants-in-chief had their own local courts, with doctors, musicians, cooks and a force of knights and soldiers.

The knight would often hold the vill from the tenant-in-chief. If he lived in the vill, he would stay in the manor house. Most of his time

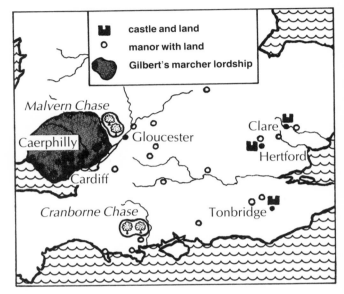

(C) Gilbert's lordship

would be spent hunting with hounds, hawking and practising fighting. He would also keep an eye on the farming of his home farm – the **demesne**. When the knight arrived in a vill he might decide to build a motte and bailey castle (see pages 26–27). This was much more likely if the vill was in an area where there was danger, like the Welsh borders. The knight could well bring his wife to live in the vill, **D**. She would run the manor house, order the servants to keep it clean and tidy and make sure fresh meat and vegetables were brought from the manor house garden or the demesne farm. The lady of the manor might also go hunting and hawking with her lord. On Holy Days she would hold a huge feast in the hall – think of the work that meant for her and her servants, and the fun they had in the evening while the feast was on.

The priest In a large vill you would find a priest, **E**. He was in charge of the local church, which the lord of the manor might have had built in stone on the site of the old Saxon wooden building. The priest's duties were to hold church services on a Sunday; to hear

(D) A knight and his lady

(E) A village priest

confession from the villagers and to give **alms** to the poor. He would also help look after the old and the sick. In the open fields you would find some strips of land for the priest to farm, his **glebe** land. The villagers would also have to pay him a tenth of what they grew and raised each year.

Other holders Although the knight was the most common holder of land from the tenant-in-chief, other men might hold vills from him. Domesday often tells us about servants of the King or tenants-in-chief who held vills. Domesday Book tells us of some of King William's servants: Nigel his doctor, the engineer who built his castles, the steersman of his boat, his interpreter, cook and treasurer.

ACTIVITY

1 Use page 6 to help you draw up a feudal pyramid of your own vill. Add to it the following people (if they were present): the King, tenant-in-chief, subholder and priest.

2 Make a large feudal pyramid of *all* the vills in your area. Then mark on the numbers of people in the pyramid: the King, tenants-in-chiefs, subholders and priests.

or Draw cutout figures of each of the characters on your feudal pyramid, and place them in a pyramid shape.

3 Draw up a table of duties of each of the people in your vill towards one another: start with King's duties to tenant-in-chief; Tenant-in-chief's duties to King; . . .

11 Steward, Reeve and Peasant

(A) A reeve overseeing peasants at work

A Domesday peasant or villein would find it strange that I own many things, such as a house and car, and can go where I like. His life was very different. The vill was the centre of his world, where he lived and worked, tied to the farming of the land.

The villein would hardly ever see the lord of his manor. Lords might have many manors hundreds of miles apart. They would employ a **steward** to look after their manors. He would travel around the manors checking they were well run.

The villeins of the manor would choose one of their fellows as **reeve** to be in charge of the manor, **A**. It was a hard job, and the reeve took the blame if things went wrong. Some peasants even paid to get out of being reeve. Others made sure their enemy got the job!

The reeve made sure the vill's rules were kept. There were many rules. You had to pay a fee or fine when you got married or when your father died and you wanted to take on his land. You had to grind your corn in the lord's mill. You had to graze your animals on the lord's land, so that they would manure it.

The reeve ran the manor court. Here he would collect money, and sort out rows over who had rights to work the land, and whether work had been done on the lord's farm.

Domesday Book gives full details of the number of peasants in each vill. It splits them into four groups: villeins; bordars; cottars and serfs (see page 25 to find out who these people were). Domesday Book gives us some clues about what village life was like. Historians can build up quite a good picture from other historical sources such as charters, court rolls (records), monks' chronicles (histories) and archaeological remains. These all help us to imagine what life as a peasant would have been like . . .

Your work changes from season to season. Most of it is out in the great open fields. There are between two and five of these. Each year one or two are left **fallow**, to get back the goodness into the soil **B**. While the fields are fallow, the animals graze on them. Great ox teams, up to eight strong, plough up the other fields **C**. Turning them round is a major job. So they plough the land in long strips – not straight, but in a long 'S' shape. At the edge of the strip the earth forms a bank (you can still see many of these 'ridge and furrow' patterns today). Some villeins have asked the manor court if they can clear waste ground for new strips. Slowly the village land is spreading. In time, a new open field may emerge.

Your life is often very harsh. If you fall ill,

© Ploughing with oxen

there are no doctors to cure you. You work long, hard hours for little reward. Your crops and animals are at the mercy of disease and the weather. Your main food is black, gritty bread made from wheat and rye, with beans, peas and ale. Sometimes a fish, taken from the stream or pond. Maybe a rabbit or deer poached from the forest. In autumn you make pots of jam from fruit and berries. From October to April you eat smoked or salted meat and fish, cooked with wild herbs.

You visit your neighbours, Jack and Joan. Their home is very like yours. It is a round, thatched hut, with mud walls and a pole holding up the roof. There is one large room.

Straw litters the floor. A fire burns on a stone hearth against one wall and the smoke escapes through a hole in the roof. Coarse bread is cooking on the heated stones around the fire. Sausages are hanging from a pole.

Joan is weaving cloth on an upright loom in the corner. A child is screaming – she is hungry, as there is little to eat. Joan goes outside to feed the chickens. Jack is out in the field, ploughing. Neither Jack nor Joan can write. On Sundays they go to mass in the church. The highlights of their year are the Holy Day feasts at Christmas and Easter, and the dancing and merriment that take place on May Day and Harvest Festival.

Ⓑ How the open fields were used

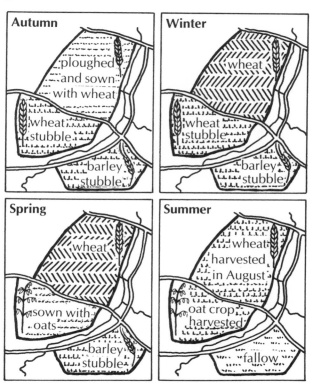

ACTIVITY

1 Draw Jack and Joan, with labels showing the jobs they are doing and what they wear.
or make up songs and sing them about peasant life.

2 The peasants' work changed through the year. Make out a table of the work they might do in each season.

3 As if you were a steward, make out the orders you would give the reeve for your vill for a week's work in April.

4 Discuss what might happen to your village if you heard a band of Danish raiders were marching towards it.

5 Hold an election to choose your vill's reeve. Then think of things you want sorted out at the first meeting of the manor court. Hold such a meeting, and produce a record (the *court roll*) of what was decided.

12 Village Crafts

The peasant needed craftsmen to make his home, tools, pots and to grind his corn. Domesday Book does not tell us much about the jobs of craftsmen. King William had no wish to know such things. In the whole of Domesday Book there is only mention of two carpenters, **A**. There must have been thousands in England. At that time nearly all buildings and all furniture were made out of wood. Now and then Domesday records a potter or smith, **B**. Can you think why both were key jobs? There are hundreds of Domesday entries about mills. Mills were a source of income for the King:

C ❨ *The Count holds Sheffield* (Sussex) *for himself. . . . 1 mill at 40d and 500 eels. Arundel Castle* (a town or borough) *. . . a mill which pays 10 measures of wheat and 10 measures of rough corn: 4 measures in addition.* ❩

A Carpenters and **B** smiths at work

Each of the mills needed a miller. Peasants hated the miller – they felt that he cheated them in grinding their corn, see page 24. Table **D** tells you more about craftsmen in the local vills.

D Men at work

> **Blacksmith** forges iron tools for the peasants, bailiff, priest and lord; the iron tip for the ploughshare; iron shoes for the horses and oxen; metal cooking pots and pans.
>
> **Carpenter** makes chairs, tables, house frames, wooden plates. Makes and repairs ploughs and the yokes for the oxen.
>
> **Potter** uses a potter's wheel to make pots and plates.
>
> **Mason** builds churches and stone manor houses. Makes millstones.
>
> **Thatcher** thatches houses, huts and barns, and haystacks. Collects bundles of dried reeds and straw for thatch.
>
> **Miller** takes charge of the lord's mill where corn is ground into flour (see page 24).

☞ ACTIVITY ☞

1 In your groups, each choose one of the craftsmen listed in **D** and draw a picture of them at work to add to your Domesday display.

2 Make out a table like the one below for your own vills.

Trade	Tools	Raw materials	Who from	What made	Who for
Blacksmith					
Carpenter					
Potter					
Mason					
Miller					

3 Our surnames today are often based on what people did in Domesday times. Work out from your class' names the kinds of jobs your ancestors *might* have done in 1086.

13 The Animals

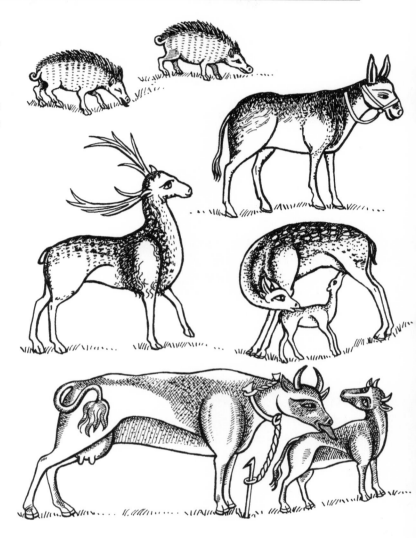

(A) 6 *Not even one ox, nor one cow, nor one pig escaped notice in his survey* (the Domesday enquiry). **9** (The Anglo-Saxon Chronicle)

Sampson (see page 13) read through the piles of replies to the King's questions (see page 10). The answers were full of facts about the animals of every vill. Too much detail, thought the abbot. So he decided to leave out the animals for most counties. Animal entries do survive for a few counties, like Devon. Look at your local Domesday entries. It is very unlikely that there will be a list of animals, but one animal which you will often find is the pig or swine. It is used to measure what the woodland is worth, as at Singleton:

(B) 6 *meadow, 60 acres. From the woodland, 150 pigs.* **9**

From what we know about Domesday England, we can make a good guess at what animals might have lived in and around your vill **C**. Let us go for a walk through the area . . . In the woodland we glimpse a herd of deer, while pigs root about or forage for food, mainly acorns. On the woodland's edge stand hives of bees. The village animals graze on the rough grassland or pasture of the common – we can see sheep, cows, goats, and donkeys. Oxen pull the ploughs in the open field, while the warhorse of the lord of the manor grazes on the meadow. Close to the lord's manor house is a dovecote – a rich supply of food in the winter. As we pass down the village street we see a peasant woman rush out with a stick, to chase away a dog from her ducks, geese, and hens. Dogs bark wildly. On the village edge we learn that eels and fish swim in the mill pool – more food for the villagers.

(C) Some of the animals in Domesday England

ACTIVITY

1 Which animals would you expect to find on the different kinds of land in your village? Add a column to your land chart (see page 17) showing these animals.

2 Make a frieze to show the animals in your vill. Add the frieze to your wall display. Also add a layer or layers of animals to your feudal pyramid diagram, see page 7.

3 What problems might we have in using the figures which Domesday provides about the animals in vills in 1086?

14 Flour, Fish and Salt

Today when you have a meal you may well eat bread with it and sprinkle salt on your food. Bread and salt mattered as much to the Normans. Domesday Book tells us if there was a **mill** in a vill or town. The grain grown on the ploughed land had to be ground into flour for making bread. It was impossible to do this by hand – although many homes kept a hand mill ready. Can you think why?

To grind their grain the Normans used the main source of power in most large vills – the stream. Beside the stream the villagers built a machine to grind corn into flour – their water mill, **A**. A mill had many parts. A waterwheel with paddles was set in the stream. To make this turn faster you would build a dam across the stream, to make a large pool of water. Then you geared the wheel to one of two millstones, which a skilled mason had cut to shape from large lumps of rock.

Mills were of great value. A miller could grind all of the vill's corn and bring in lots of money. The lord of the manor might own the mill, or the villeins might join in a club to build a shared mill. Then, they would also share out the profits. We know one man had a fourth share every third year. A long time to wait for his profit – but a very nice windfall when it came. A vill might contain mills to grind the corn from other vills. Battersea in Surrey had seven mills which brought in one third of the manor's income.

The villeins caught fish and eels from the mill ponds. The Normans loved eels and ate them by the thousand. Fish was a great source of food. As winter drew on, supplies of salt meat grew low and stinking. The church said people should stop eating meat *(fast)* at this time, and eat fish instead. Villagers dug fish ponds and used the mill pool. They also set fish traps at weirs – Tiddenham had 60 salmon traps.

If you had been a Norman you would have used salt to make your food taste better – as we do today. You also needed tons of salt to keep meat and fish in barrels through the winter (no deep freezers in those days!). The Normans were very good at making salt. Near the coast they used sea water. Inland they made salt 'wiches' (like Droitwich). They put the salt-laden water *(brine)* into pits. The water evaporated, leaving the salt behind. Or, they heated brine up in huge lead pans and drove off the water in that way. In Sussex there are numerous entries which tell us of the making of salt in Norman times. Typical was the entry for the vill of Hailsham, part of a larger manor.

B ❝ *2 salt-houses at 7s*
In this manor the Count kept
11 salt-houses, value 24s 6d. ❞

Salt-making was big business. So was sending the salt to every vill in England. Place-names with 'sal' or 'salt' in them may tell us that salt merchants used that place to sell their salt in Norman times.

ACTIVITY

1 Design a mill for your vill. See if you can make a working model. Discuss how the Normans might build their mill, and what *crafts* were needed to build a mill like **A**.

2 Look at Domesday Book for your area to find out which vills had mills. Mark where they were – or might have been – on a local map.

3 Use a *gazetteer* for your area to work out places where salt merchants might have traded. Here's one to start off – Salford, the ford in the river where they took the salt carts across. *Or* Look at a map of Britain to find places with 'sal' in them.

A A water mill

15 Counting People and Animals

Now and then Domesday Book mentions women and children. Most of the time the commissioners only put down the men who worked in the field and forest. So, when they put down figures like 'there are 11 villeins' we must add their families to them to get the number of people in a vill. To do this, multiply by five. How many people does this give us? In this way you can find out how many people might have lived on your manor.

In Domesday Book you will find strange names. What they meant often changed from one place to another. What a muddle! The *definitions* below are a rough guide to working out what the men in your vill were like.

First of all there were the **freemen** or **sokemen** – about 1 in 6 of the people. There were a lot in the Danelaw. Freemen were *free* to leave the vill if they wished. This did not mean they were rich, that is, owned a lot of land. Today all of us over 18-years-old are freemen – and many of us are poor!

Next come the **villeins**, **bordars**, **cottars** and **coscets**. They made up 3 out of 4 of the population. A typical **villein** might have 30 acres of land. But, he would have to serve his lord (do **boon service**) by ploughing the lord's land, cutting his hay and harvesting his crops. He would also have to pay dues or rent for using his woods to pasture pigs. Some villeins were rich, and just paid their lord money instead of doing boon work.

A **bordar** was the same as a villein, with much less land – about five acres. The bordars would have to work on the villein's land to make a living.

Cottars and **coscets** only had their huts (cots) and gardens.

The worst off were the **serfs** – 1 in 10 of the population. They were slaves. In their own time they could earn money, and if they saved up they could even buy their own freedom. There were few serfs in the Danelaw (see page 2).

To count the animals in a vill, allow four to eight oxen for each plough. The lord would own his own oxen – the peasants would have to club together to make up an ox team. There were lots of cows. Domesday Book mentions dairy farms and cheese. There were huge flocks of *sheep* **A** – up to 1000 strong.

(A) Sheep in a sheepfold

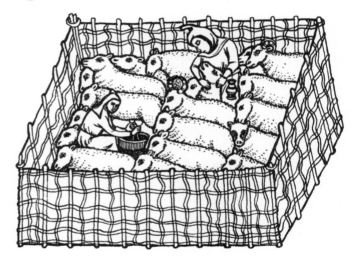

ACTIVITY

1 Use the figures here to work out who might have lived in your vill: the number of people or families in each group. Also see how much land they farmed. Add up what the vill or town was worth. Add this to your feudal pyramid.

2 Plan out the fields for your vill.
   a Talk about where the strips of the lord and peasants might be. Each strip was one acre – a day's ploughing.
   b Put the strips in on the map, with a key to show who owned what.
   c Plan out the year's farming, see page 16.

16 The Castle

Look back at pages 4–5. William's greatest problem was how he, with some 4000–5000 Normans, was going to control the 1.25 million Anglo-Saxons.

Imagine you are one of Gilbert of Clare's knights (see page 18). You live in a vill on the Welsh border. You and your two Norman foot-soldiers are a day's ride from the nearest Norman knight. A band of Welsh raiders is on the rampage. The local villagers might slit your throat in the night – they loved their Anglo-Saxon lord, who was cut down at Hastings. You cannot even trust the local peasant girl who shares your bed and cooks your food. How do you feel on dark, stormy nights, when the wind howls through the thatch, the house beams creak and groan, and the dogs bark wildly outside?

From Normandy you would have brought a simple idea to protect you – the **castle**. It was a new idea; in 1066 there were only one or two in England. The castle started out as a base from which knights on horseback (cavalry) could control the local vills. On horseback, a knight could reach the enemy much quicker than on foot. Because the knight was sitting high up, he could beat down men on foot with his sword or club. The knights needed somewhere to stable their horses, keep supplies of hay, store weapons

and live and sleep. So they thought of the castle.

The first castle was a deep ditch, dug around quite a big area. Inside the ditch the earth was thrown up to make a high bank. On top of the bank was a high wooden fence. The fence posts were sharpened into points. Inside, there would be huts and stables. All this was called a **bailey**.

You would probably feel quite safe inside your strong bailey. But what if the enemy attacked and shinned over the fence? Where could you retreat to? The Normans had the answer. Inside the bailey they would build a huge mound of earth, or **motte**. On top, they put a fence and a watch tower. So if an enemy band got into the bailey, you could climb up a ladder into the tower, and then pull up the ladder and defend yourself.

Think how much safer you would have felt guarding the Welsh borders from your motte and bailey castle, **A**.

The Normans built their castles in towns along major routeways, and at crossroads. A knight would build a castle to protect his manors. Only a few castles were built in stone, like **A**. Most earth mottes could not take the weight of a stone tower, until the earth had time to settle down.

Ⓐ A motte and bailey castle (most had wooden towers and walls)

King William's castles showed the Anglo-Saxons how strong he was. You can still see William's London castle today, very much as he built it: it is the White Tower inside the Tower of London. It is built of stone. William lived at his castles. The White Tower is partly a royal palace. You can see the great store-rooms on the ground floor; the King's hall – for feasting, council meetings and law courts; the royal bedroom (where the King kept his jewels and gold) and the royal chapel.

By 1086 there were hundreds of Norman motte and bailey castles, **B**. Domesday Book only tells us of about 50. Mostly they are mentioned in passing, as at Shrewsbury, when townspeople protested about paying taxes for houses which had been demolished to build the castle. At Eastbourne, near Hastings, we learn of another castle when Domesday Book mentions:

Ⓒ ❛ *William holds 1 hide of this land. Alfred 1 hide, the Castle warden 2 hides . . .* ❜

William did not want to put castles down in Domesday Book. Castles did not make him any money, so there was no need to count them, or to find out what they were worth.

ACTIVITY

1 Look at the map on page 3. Work out reasons why William would have built castles at the places shown. Take care to look at different areas.

2 a In your groups, discuss where you might choose to place a castle. Think of the points you would take into account – roads, water, height, position of other vills.

b When you have agreed on a site, plan out how you would build your castle. Work out what buildings you would need, the stores they would contain, the plan of your castle, how you would get it built – raw materials, craftsmen, workers and so on. Use **B** to help you.

c Make a model of your castle *or* work out a board game using attackers and defenders to see how your castle might fare if a band of 20 Anglo-Saxon raiders attacked it, and you and two other Normans defended it.

Ⓑ Plan of a Norman castle

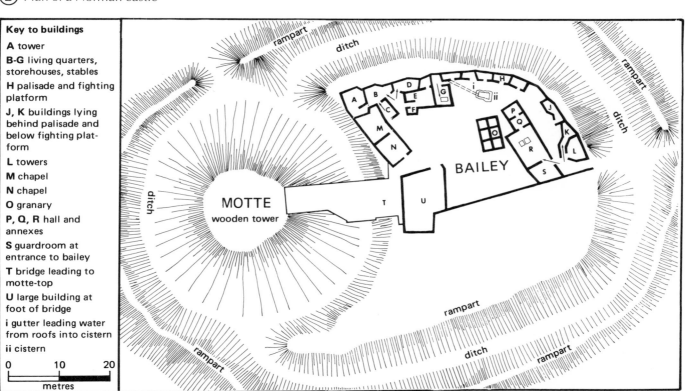

Key to buildings

A tower

B-G living quarters, storehouses, stables

H palisade and fighting platform

J, K buildings lying behind palisade and below fighting platform

L towers

M chapel

N chapel

O granary

P, Q, R hall and annexes

S guardroom at entrance to bailey

T bridge leading to motte-top

U large building at foot of bridge

i gutter leading water from roofs into cistern

ii cistern

0   10   20
metres

MOTTE
wooden tower

BAILEY

17 The Church

William the Conqueror had a strong belief in God. To William the victory at Hastings was God's work. After the battle William and his army may have sunk to its knees in prayer, holding aloft its banner the Pope had blessed. On the site where King Harold had died William built Battle Abbey. Its monks prayed for the souls of both English and Norman soldiers killed in the battle.

In England William found that the Anglo-Saxons had strong Christian beliefs, with their own saints and shrines. There was a rich Anglo-Saxon church. It owned one-sixth of the country's wealth. Churches and cathedrals had grown up without any plan or pattern. The Pope in Italy, and not the Anglo-Saxon King, ran the church **A**. William was going to change all that, with the help of Lanfranc, his new Italian Archbishop of Canterbury. It would become William's church, although it would still look to the Pope for guidance over Christian prayer and beliefs. William and Lanfranc attacked on two fronts: the monasteries or nunneries and the bishoprics. Domesday Book contains many clues about what happened to the lands of both the monasteries and the bishoprics.

Between 1066 and 1085 monasteries and nunneries had grown, and new ones had been set up, **B**. William decided to place them under the control of Norman monasteries. The Norman monasteries were part of much larger

Ⓒ A monk at work

European communities or orders of monks. The monks prayed for all sinners who lived in the outside world. They believed this would help sinners go to heaven when they died — like a 'piggy bank' of saved-up prayers. The monasteries helped the poor, the sick and the old. They were places to study and to teach **C**. Monks and nuns played a key job in helping local villagers. See how much of your local land abbeys owned.

Tackling the bishoprics was just as big a job. Often they were centred on small Anglo-Saxon vills, or a long way from the bulk of lands they owned. The diocese of Lincoln's lands stretched from the Humber to the Thames, but its bishop was based in Dorchester!

William and Lanfranc moved the bishoprics into the towns. There they built great stone cathedrals; with massive pillars and rich stone carvings. They must have seemed like skyscrapers to the Anglo-Saxons! What a contrast to their own ramshackle buildings of wood and mud, with thatch roofs. The cathedrals cost huge amounts of money. Often the builders were not skilled enough. Many of their towers fell down. But they went on building and rebuilding, for the Norman bishop was a great man. He felt that his glory and power would be shown in the glory he could give to God through a great building.

William and Lanfranc chose Normans to be their new bishops. Some of the bishops were devout religious men. Others were great barons. The Bishop of Durham was the great feudal

Ⓐ The Norman church

THE NORMAN CHURCH

The Pope He was the representative of God on Earth. He was very powerful and everyone obeyed him on questions of faith.

Archbishops and Bishops They were often rich and powerful. They owned a lot of land. They spent much time advising the King.

The Parish Priests They were very poor and did most of the hard work.

lord of the area. William's half brother Odo, Bishop of Bayeux, fought at Hastings alongside William. Soon Odo was made Earl of Kent.

The bishops and abbots owed William feudal service, just like any other great lords. They had to give him knights. Domesday Book tells us the service they owed to the King.

In your vill there could well be a village priest. There was one priest for about six vills. Domesday Book mentions 2061 churches. The entry for Singleton is like hundreds of others:

(D) ‹ *A church in whose (lands) lie 3 hides and 1 virgate of this land. The clergy have 2 ploughs and 5 villeins . . .* ›

The churches made money, which was split up among many people. The priest would get some of the cash. He might keep the fees for marriages and funerals. The church tax or **tithe** – one-tenth of every man's income – often went to the person who had founded the church (paid for it to be built). The village land set aside to support the church (**glebe** land) was often large and made lots of money.

ACTIVITY

1 Use Domesday Book to find out:
  a where were the abbeys and bishoprics in your area?
  b what lands did they own?
  c how was the money for the church in any of your vills split up?
Add these facts about the church's lands to your feudal pyramid for the country, or for your vill.

2 If in 1086 you were to talk to the following, what might they tell you about their lives, and how things had changed in their vill, monastery or bishopric since 1066:
  a a *monk*, who had been at Battle Abbey, on the site of the Battle of Hastings, from the moment William had said he would build it?
  b a *priest*, who had been in his vill since 1064?
  c the Anglo-Saxon Bishop of Worcester, whom William allowed to remain as bishop after the conquest?

(B) A monastery

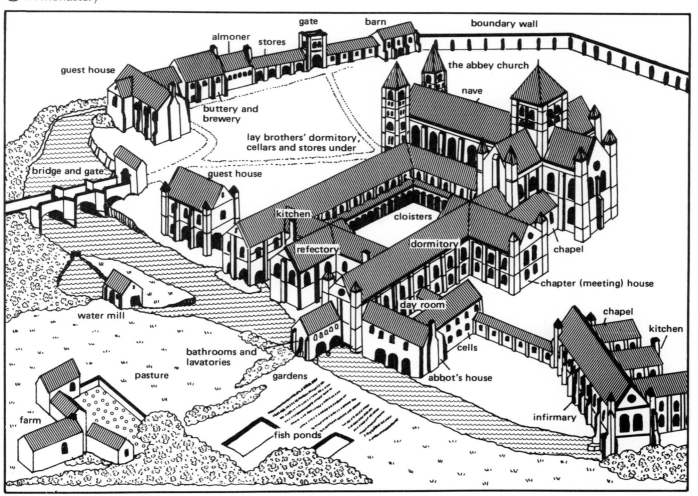

18 Towns and Fairs

Today most of us live in towns. In 1086 only a tiny proportion of the people had their homes in a town. Still, towns played an important part in Norman life. A town then had much the same role or job as one today. It was a *market place* for goods grown or made in the vills in the area it served; a centre of *industry* where craftsmen had workshops to make goods to sell; a place which provided *services* the area needed. These might include *religion* (the cathedral and bishop's palace); *justice* (the King's law courts); *defence* (the King's castle); and *government* (the King's tax collector).

Towns were rich. Domesday entries help us work out what they were like. Let us try to unpick the meaning of a typical entry – that for Chester. The entry is very long. So, we will look at key parts.

Domesday Chester

The city of Chester paid geld (**1**) T.R.E. (**2**) for 50 hides (**3**). There are 3½ hides (**3**) which are outside the city, that is 1½ hides beyond the bridge (**4**) and 2 hides in Newton (**5**), and Red Cliff and in the bishop's borough (**6**) these paid geld (**1**) with the city.

There were in the T.R.E. (**2**), 431 houses which paid geld (**1, 6**). This city then paid 10½ marks of silver (**7**). Two-thirds went to the King and one-third to the earl. These were the laws which were then observed (**8**).

(Some examples . . .)

He who killed a man on these holydays (**9**) paid a fine of 4 pounds (**10**) but on other days 40 shillings (**11**). He who failed to take part in a hue and cry (**12**) in the city paid 10 shillings.

He who wished to take over the land of a relative gave 10 shillings, and if he could not or would not pay this, the reeve (**13**) took his land into the King's land.

If a ship came against the King's peace, and despite his ban, the King and the earl had the ship . . . (**14**).

A man or a woman caught giving false measure (**15**) paid a fine of 4 shillings, likewise the maker of bad beer (**16**) was either set in the ducking stool (**17**), or paid 4 shillings to the reeves.

There was in this city T.R.E. 7 moneyers (**18**).

There were then 12 'judges' of the city (**19**). If any of them absented themselves from the hundred court . . . (**20**).

For the repair of the city wall (**21**), the reeve was wont to call up one man from each side in the courts.

When Earl Hugh received it, it was not worth more than 30 pounds for it was greatly wasted (**22**). There were 205 houses less than there had been T.R.E. There are now the same number as he found there.

As well as going to towns' markets, Normans would meet to buy and sell their produce at markets or fairs held in certain vills. A vill might only have its market on one day of the year.

Domesday Book may not contain the entry for your local town. The entry for England's largest town, London, is missing.

Sorting Out a Town's Entry:

First Look in the *Index*, inside the back cover, to find the meaning of any terms in your entries you do not know.

Second Work through the Chester entry. It gives you an idea of how you can work out what a local town was like.

Chester Number	Notes	Index
1	Geld – tax paid.	9
2	T.R.E. – Before 1066 (Time of King (Rex) Edward).	2
3	Hides – land measurement.	14
4	Bridge – the town bridge over the river.	
5	Newton – A new town, outside the town walls.	

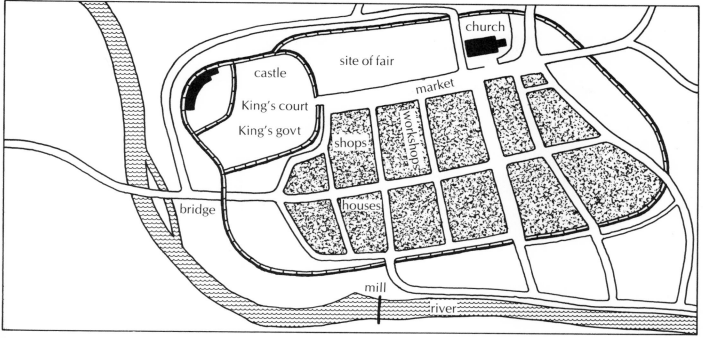

(B) Town plan

Chester Number	Notes	Index
6	Bishop's borough. The bishop's own town – a rival to Chester.	28
7	Mark – coinage.	
8	*Laws* – the town would have its own laws for running its affairs.	
9	Holy days. The city would have 'holydays' on Saints' days.	21
10, 11	Pounds and shillings – money.	
12	Hue and cry. Chasing a thief to arrest him.	
13	Reeve – The king's or earl's man who ran the town.	20
14	Evidence about the port, and piracy?	
15	False amounts or weights of goods.	
16	Evidence of town crafts and traders.	
17	A Norman punishment.	
18	Makers of coins – the town had a mint.	
19, 20	The town's court.	
21	Hundred – the area of the county.	10
22	Wasting.	15
23	The city had a wall.	

ACTIVITY

1 What things might you be able to buy, and what services would there be for you to use in Norman:

  a London;

  b Lincoln;

  c A small town near your school;

  d A large vill near your school.

2 In groups try to work out what your local Domesday town might have been like. Either take your nearest Domesday town entry, or use the suggestions below to create your own town.

  a *The Laws.* At a meeting draw up a list of *laws* you need for the running of your town.

  b *The court.* Choose 12 court members to try cases which members of your town have brought against one another.

  c *The town plan.* Draw up a plan of what the town might have been like (see **B**). Put on where these *might* have been: town walls, towers, gates; main streets; shops and houses; castle; bishop's palace; market square; church; bridges; mill.

  d You can give the roles of townspeople to class members. In groups, bargain with each other over the sale or exchange of goods and services. Each person can have *10* units of goods: bread; coins; fish; chairs; defence; law . . . Exchange your units by *bargaining* until you have what you need to survive.

19 Domesday Today

What might someone in a 1000 years time like to know about you, your friends, the lives you live and the world you live in? Prepare a set of questions like those William asked about England in 1086. To do this, each of you draw up a list of questions. You can then sort these out under headings as a questionnaire. Below is the questionnaire my class worked out.

DOMESDAY TODAY – 1985 QUESTIONNAIRE

PERSONAL
1 What time do you get up?
2 Do you go to bed early?
3 Do you break the law?
4 How much pocket money do you get, and what do you spend it on?
5 Do you own a watch/musical instrument/computer?
6 Do you have a television/telephone?

FAMILY
7 At what age did your parents leave school/home?
8 What job or jobs does your father and/or mother do?
9 Are your parents divorced or remarried?
10 Does your father buy a new vehicle yearly and why?
11 Is swearing accepted in your family?

JOBS/EMPLOYMENT
12 What do you want to do when you are old enough?
13 Do you have a Saturday/after school job?
14 Do you run your own business?

PETS/ANIMALS
15 Do you have animals?
16 If so, what kind?
17 Do you like animals?

LEISURE
18 What do you do in your spare time?
19 Do you go to a youth club/pub/restaurant?
20 What books do you read?

SCHOOL/EDUCATION
21 What kind of subjects do you take at school?
22 Do you agree with homework, and how much do you do?
23 How far do you go to school, and do you walk?

TRAVEL
24 If you had a choice, where would you most like to visit, and why?
25 Do you go abroad for your holiday?

THE HOME
26 Do you live in a house/bungalow/flat?
27 How many people live in your house? Who are they?
28 Do you have a garden, if so, how big?

RELIGION
29 Are you religious – do you have any 'religious' beliefs?
30 Do you go to church?

LANGUAGES
31 What languages do you speak?

FOOD
32 What is your favourite meal?
33 What did you eat for breakfast?

COMPUTERS
34 What kind of computers do you have?
35 How many people have computers?
36 Do you own a computer?

THE MEDIA
37 What is your favourite TV programme?
38 What TV and radio programmes do you watch and listen to?

POLITICS
39 Do you support Conservative, Labour, Liberal or SDP?
40 Do you support CND?

GENERAL
41 Who is your favourite famous person? Why do you like him/her?
42 Do you like all members of the royal family?
43 What kind of weather do you like?
44 Do you ever use public transport?
45 Have you ever broken any bones?
46 Any other serious injury?
47 What is the crime rate in your area?
48 Does anyone in your family drink heavily?
49 Are you mature?